Making Moving Pictures

David Wickers
and
Sharon Finmark

Studio Vista

Cassell Australia

A Studio Vista/Cassell Australia book

Published in Great Britain by
Studio Vista a division of
Cassell and Collier Macmillan Publishers Limited
35 Red Lion Square, London WC1R 4SG

Sydney, Auckland, Toronto, Johannesburg
an affiliate of the Macmillan Publishing Co. Inc.
New York
and in Australia by
Cassell Australia Limited
31 Bridge Road, Stanmore, New South Wales
30 Curzon Street, North Melbourne, Victoria.

Text copyright © 1972, 1976 David Wickers and Sharon Finmark
Illustrations copyright © 1972, 1976 Studio Vista
Adapted from: How to Make your own kinetics

First published in this edition 1976

Printed in Great Britain
by Purnell & Sons Ltd., Paulton (Avon) and London

ISBN (Great Britain) 0 289 70709 9
ISBN (Australia) 0 7269 9256 9

Contents

Introduction

The world in which we live is full of moving objects of one kind or another. Motor cars are driven along our streets, birds fly overhead, the television brings moving pictures to our homes.

This book is also about moving objects. If you paint a picture or make a clay model it will stay exactly the same once it is finished. But you can make moving pictures called Kinetics. They change all the time as you watch them or play with them and they seem almost to come alive.

You do not need expensive motors or complicated electrical power to make Kinetics work. By using such everyday objects as coloured paper, oil, water, mirrors, beads, magnets and plastic bags you can easily make your own moving world.

Flowering spiral

You need:
white card
compasses
a thick, black felt marker
a sheet of acetate or thick cellophane
scissors
ruler
pencil
drawing pin

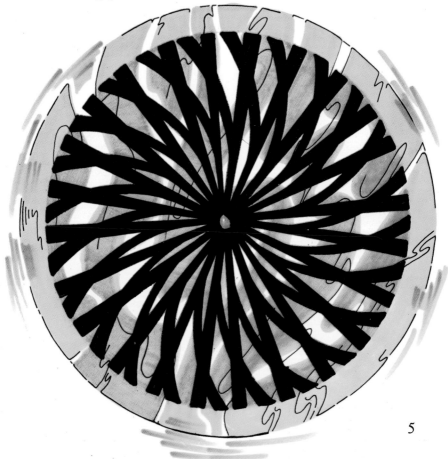

1 Draw a large circle on the card, making the radius at least 12cm (5in). Keep the compasses set at the same radius and put the point anywhere on the edge of the circle. Draw a curve from the edge of the circle to the centre.

2 Put the point of the compasses where this curve touches the edge of the circle and draw another curve to the centre. Repeat this all the way round the circle.

3 Put the point of the compasses on the edge of the circle half way between two of the curves. Continue round the circle in the same way as before. Repeat this until you have drawn 24 curves.

4 Blacken and thicken the lines with a felt marker.

5 Draw on the acetate a circle with the same radius as the first one. Keeping the point of the compasses where it is, draw a second, larger circle on the acetate. Lay the acetate over the card and mark on it the 24 points where the curves touch the edge of the smaller circle. With the felt marker draw a straight line from each point to the centre of the acetate circle.

6 Cut round the edge of the card circle and round the larger acetate circle. Lay the acetate on the card. Push a drawing pin through the centre of both circles and pin them to the wall. Turn the acetate slowly round and round.

The two sets of lines will move like a never-ending spiral when you rotate the top sheet. This is a moiré.

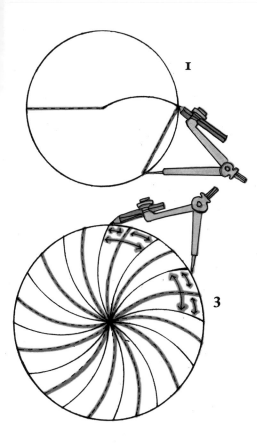

I

2

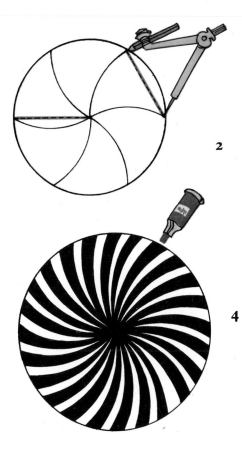

3

4

5

6

Prison bars

You need:
corrugated cardboard
a piece of white card
ruler and pencil
needle and cotton
glue
drawing pins
scissors
black and white paint

1 Paint the corrugated cardboard white. When it is dry, paint the raised stripes black (or use a broad felt-tipped pen instead).

2 Draw lines on the white card the same distance apart as the width of the stripes on the corrugated cardboard.

3 Cut a strip off the bottom of the card and put it on one side.

4 Cut along the lines you have drawn, leaving a margin on all three sides. Cut across the top of alternate stripes and remove them completely. Take the piece of card you set aside and glue it to the bottoms of the strips that are left. This will make the fourth side of a frame.

8

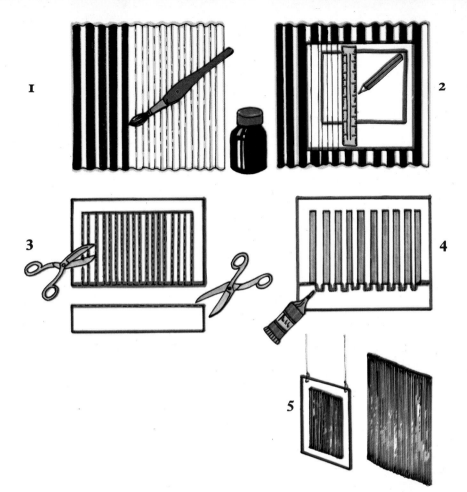

5 Pin the corrugated card to the wall. Thread some cotton through the two top corners of the card frame and hang it from the ceiling with drawing pins. It should hang about 30cm (12in) in front of the corrugated card and be tilted to one side.

As you walk past the 'prison bars' their effect on your eyes may make you feel a little dizzy. This is called a moiré. You can discover similar vibrating effects by laying pieces of metal gauze or net curtains on top of each other and watching the patterns that form when you move or turn them.

Film show

You need:
2 round cardboard cake
   stands or boxes
a large nail
a large bead
thin card
black paint
felt-tipped pens
scissors
roll of narrow gummed
   paper
drawing pins
ruler

1 Cut a piece of card 15cm (or 6in) wide and long enough to wrap once around a cake stand. (You may have to join two pieces of card together.) Cut 12 evenly spaced slits in the card. They should be 6·5 (or 2½in) deep and just under 50mm (¼in) wide.

2 Stick a strip of gummed paper all along the top of the slits and paint one side of the card black.

3 On the other side of the card draw your 'filmstar' in 12 different but connected positions. One figure should come directly beneath each slit. Do not let them come right to the bottom of the card. Try drawing a juggler tossing balls into the air.

4 Pin the card round the edge of one cake stand so that the figures face inwards. Find the centre point of the second cake stand by balancing it on the point of the nail. Push the nail right through and thread the bead

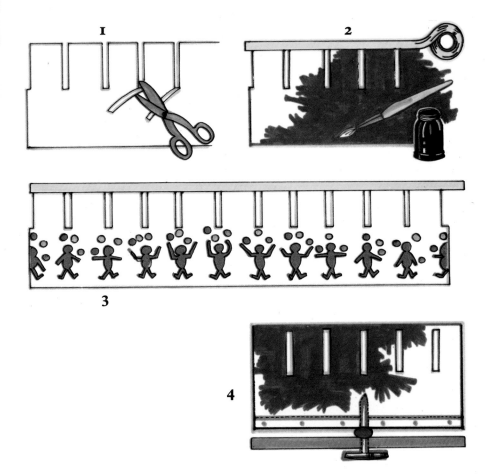

onto it. Now push the nail right through the centre of the first cake stand.

When you spin the 'film show' round and look through the slits, the juggler will seem to be tossing the balls into the air. Try drawing other film shows in the same way.

Magic pendulum

You need:
a rectangular piece of
    white card
red cellophane paper
needle and cotton
adhesive tape
crayons
drawing pins

1 Cut a frame from around the edge of the card and put it to one side.

2 Draw a vase on the remaining part of the card using any colour except red. Now add some flowers in red crayon. (The shade of red should be the same as that of the red cellophane.)

3 Tightly cover the card frame with red cellophane and stick it down with adhesive tape. Using the needle

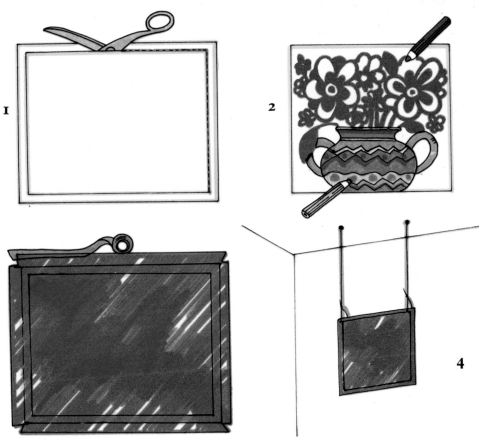

to help you, thread a length of cotton through each of the two top corners of the frame. Tie the cotton firmly to the card. Pin the other ends of the cotton to the ceiling so that the frame hangs close to the wall.

4 Pin the picture to the wall directly behind the red cellophane frame.

Start the 'pendulum' frame swaying, and you won't believe your own eyes. The flowers will disappear completely when the red cellophane passes over the picture! You could make other trick pictures in this way – a man with a red dog, a street with a red bus, or Santa Claus sitting on a heap of toys.

Unidentified flying objects

You need:
8 'flat' magnets (not the
    horseshoe type)
thin fishing line or cotton
8 empty household
    containers (4 small,
    4 medium-sized)
a large cardboard box
a piece of fabric
coloured paper or paint
glue
scissors
matches

1 Arrange the magnets in pairs. Mark those sides that repel or push each other away when held together.

2 Glue each of the magnets on top of a container so that the marked sides face upwards.

3 Cut out one large side of the box. Glue the four largest containers on the base.

4 Attach a piece of fishing line about 60cm (or 24in) long to each of the small containers. Do this by removing the lid, making a hole in the centre with a needle, threading the fishing line through, and knotting the end round a piece of matchstick. Replace the lid.

5 Hang the small containers to the 'roof' of the box by making four small holes and attaching the fishing line in the same way as before. The magnets on the small containers should hang right above those on the larger

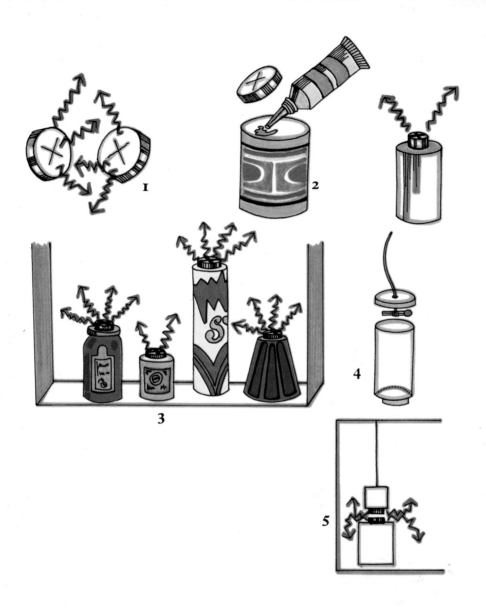

ones. The pair of magnets should come as near as possible without touching.

Hide the containers by laying the piece of fabric over them. The U.F.O.'s will hover above the ground in a very mysterious way, just like space craft.

Magnetic maze

You need:
the lid of a large cardboard
    box
iron filings
a strong magnet
strips of balsa wood
scissors
adhesive tape
4 cotton reels or spools
cellophane paper
paint

1 Paint the inside of the lid a bright colour. When it is dry, glue strips of balsa wood onto the inside of the lid at all kinds of angles to each other.

2 Glue a cotton reel or spool to each of the four corners of the other side of the lid.

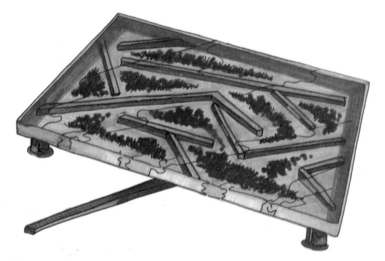

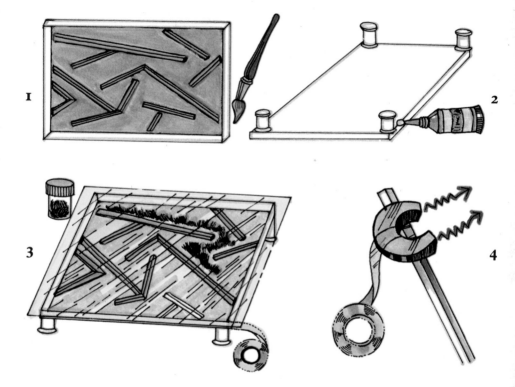

3 Put some iron filings in the lid and cover it with a sheet of cellophane paper. Stick the paper to the edges of the lid with adhesive tape.

4 Attach the magnet to a fairly thick strip of balsa wood by binding it to the end with adhesive tape.

Move the magnet around underneath the lid. You will find that the iron filings will be attracted to the magnet and follow it through the maze like an army of live insects on the march.

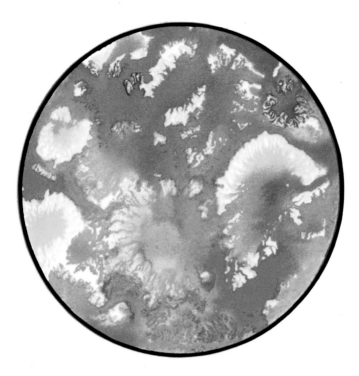

Exploding colours

You need:
artificial food dyes
large pan or dish
washing-up liquid
   (liquid detergent)
milk

1 Pour some milk into the dish. It should be about 1·5cm($\frac{1}{2}$in) deep.

2 Sprinkle a few drops of different coloured food dyes gently on the surface of the milk. You could use coloured inks instead, but the effect will not be as good.

1   2

3 Carefully let a drop of the liquid detergent run down the side of the dish. It will sink beneath the surface of the milk.

3

After a short while the detergent will make the colours move around in all directions. This swirling effect will last several minutes, forming many beautiful patterns. You can change the direction of the movements by adding more detergent to the other side of the dish.

Spin-a-disc

You need:
thick card
powder paints
string
pointed scissors
glue
compasses

1 Draw a circle with a radius of about 4cm ($1\frac{1}{2}$in) on the card and cut it out.

2 Cut small triangular 'teeth' all round the edge.

3 Make two small holes in the middle of the card using the point of the compasses. Cut a small piece of card to fit in between these holes and glue it on. This will make the holes stronger.

4 Divide one side of the card into three equal areas. Paint one area bright red, another yellow, and the third blue.

5 Paint a line of coloured spots on the other side of the card. Paint a blue spot at each end of the cardboard strip, a red spot at the top edge of the card and also at the bottom edge, and a yellow spot between them.

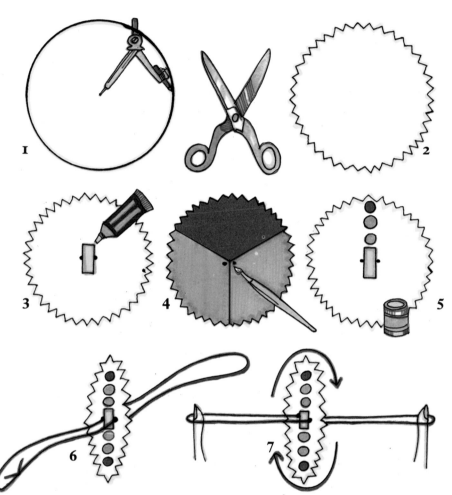

6 Thread a piece of string about 1·5m (5ft) long through one hole and back through the other. Tie the ends together to make a loop.

7 Slip a finger through each end of the loop and wind up the spin-a-disc by twisting it round and round.

When you pull the string the spin-a-disc will whoosh through the air and wind itself up again. The spots will become rings of colour and the red, yellow and blue areas will merge to become white!

Kaleidoscope

You need:
2 pieces of mirror about
    20cm × 4cm
    (8½in × 1½in)
thin cardboard
coloured gummed paper
adhesive tape
small plastic bag
greaseproof paper
scissors

1 Place two mirrors side by side facing inwards. Join them together along the top with adhesive tape.

2 Cut a strip of cardboard 2·5cm (1in) wide and the same length as the mirrors. Use adhesive tape to join its long edges to the mirrors to form a triangular column.

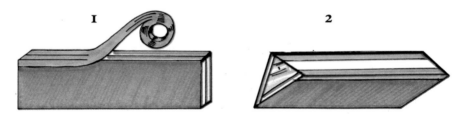

1   **2**

3 Roll a piece of cardboard into a tube around the mirrors so that they are firmly held inside. Stick it down with adhesive tape.

4 Stick a piece of plastic over one end of the tube. On the other end stick a circle of card with a peephole cut in the middle.

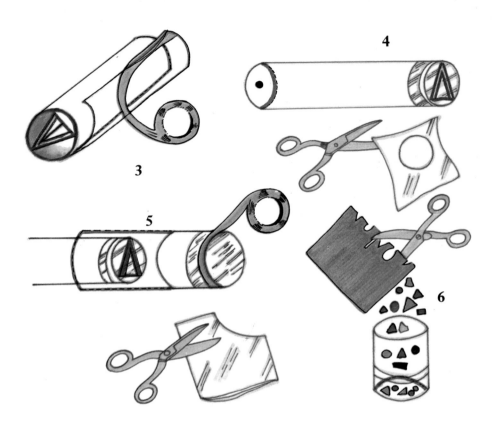

5 Wrap a piece of cardboard about 5cm (2in) wide tightly round the tube. Tape the ends together to make a second, shorter tube and slide it off the longer one. Stick some greaseproof paper over one end.

6 Glue some pieces of gummed paper back to back so that both sides are coloured, and cut out several small shapes. Put them inside the shorter tube. Slide this shorter tube back onto the longer one. Decorate the whole kaleidoscope with gummed paper shapes.

You will see all kinds of patterns when you turn the end of the kaleidoscope. You could experiment with small beads or sequins or other small objects instead of paper shapes.

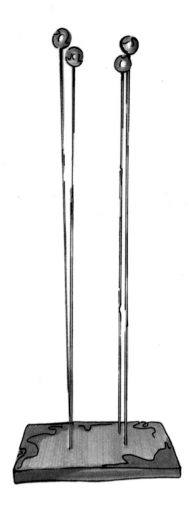

Swaying antennae

You need:
4 ping-pong balls
4 lengths of medium gauge
   piano wire 30cm (3ft)
   long (from craft
   shops)
glue
hammer
pincers
1 small nail (or panel pin)
a block of wood
enamel paint

1 Make four holes in the wooden block with the small nail, removing the nail each time with the pincers.

2 Glue a piece of wire into each of the holes.

3 Put a dab of glue on top of each wire. Push each one through a ping-pong ball until it touches the far side of the ball.

4 Carefully paint the balls and the base.

24

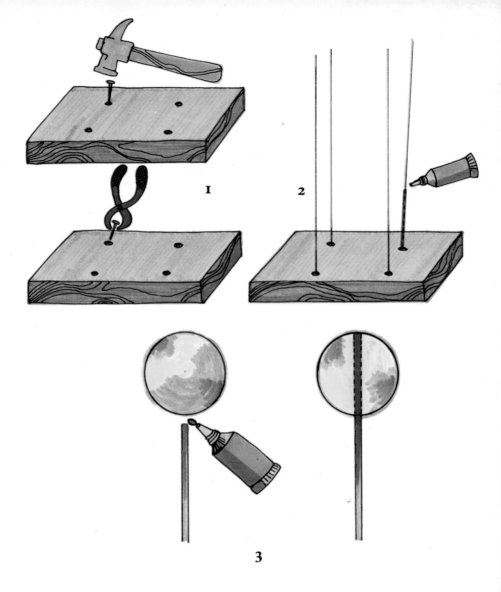

Once the glue has set you will be able to start the antennae swaying through the air. You may like to put them outside the house – in a window-box, perhaps – so that they will move in the wind. Try out different objects on the ends of the wire, and try changing the length of the wires to alter their sway.

Soft feely box

You need:
a large cardboard box
wire
small plastic bags
cotton wool
a sheet of foam rubber
glue
adhesive tape
scissors
paints or coloured paper

1 Cut a hole in the end of the box large enough for your hand to pass through.

2 Glue the foam rubber to the inside of the box, including the lid. Where the rubber covers the hand-hole, cut two slits in the shape of a cross.

3 Blow up the plastic bags and twist some wire around each opening so that the air does not escape.

4 Arrange the bags in the box and add balls of cotton wool to fill up the spaces.

5 Seal down the lid with adhesive tape and decorate the box with coloured paper or paint.

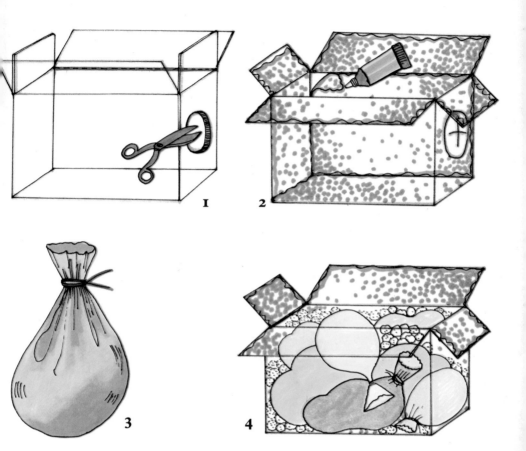

When you put your hand into the box everything you feel will be soft. Give it to your friends to try without telling them what is inside. You could make a whole series of feely boxes, each one having its own special 'feelings'. Use objects like stones, little boxes, and even cornflakes to make a hard feely box, or lots of cotton and elastic bands stretched from side to side for a stringy feely box . . . or whatever you can think of.

Index